whoopie pies

whoopie pies

A collection of delicious sweet treats

LOVE FOOD™

This edition published in 2011
LOVE FOOD is an imprint of Parragon Books Ltd

Parragon
Queen Street House
4 Queen Street
Bath BA1 1HE, UK

www.parragon.com

ISBN: 978-1-4454-6404-6

Printed in China

Written by Angela Drake
Photography by Clive Streeter
Home economy and food styling by Angela Drake

Notes for the Reader
This book uses both metric and imperial measurements. Follow the same
units of measurement throughout; do not mix metric and imperial. All spoon
measurements are level: teaspoons are assumed to be 5 ml, and tablespoons are
assumed to be 15 ml. Unless otherwise stated, milk is assumed to be full fat, eggs
and individual vegetables are medium, and pepper is freshly ground black pepper.

The times given are an approximate guide only. Preparation times differ according
to the techniques used by different people and the cooking times may also vary
from those given. Optional ingredients, variations or serving suggestions have not
been included in the calculations.

Recipes using raw or very lightly cooked eggs should be avoided by infants, the
elderly, pregnant women, convalescents and anyone suffering from an illness.
Pregnant and breastfeeding women are advised to avoid eating peanuts and
peanut products. Sufferers from nut allergies should be aware that some of the
ready-made ingredients used in the recipes in this book may contain nuts. Always
check the packaging before use.

Contents

JUST WHAT IS A WHOOPIE PIE?

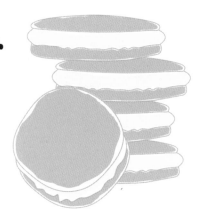

Simple to make and delicious to eat, a whoopie pie is two soft mounds of cake sandwiched together with a creamy filling to make a perfect hand-held sweet treat!

The whoopie pie originates from New England and Pennsylvania and legend has it that its name comes from the cry of 'Whoopie!' that farmers or children would shout when they opened their lunchboxes and found one nestling inside.

The traditional and original whoopie pie consists of two dark and moist chocolate cakes filled with a generous amount of creamy white marshmallow frosting. Other classic flavours include vanilla, pumpkin, chocolate chip and gingerbread, but there's no limit to the variety of flavours and fillings that can be created. In this book you'll find a huge selection of whoopie pie recipes ranging from classic favourites to deliciously overindulgent versions for extra special occasions. You don't need to have the skills of a master baker to produce great whoopie pies and you'll find that once you enter the world of whoopie pie making there'll be no going back!

EQUIPMENT YOU WILL NEED

Baking sheets – it's worth investing in 2–3 large good quality baking sheets for making whoopie pies. As a general guide you'll only be able to fit 8–10 mounds of the batter on each sheet (more for the mini-sized whoopies) as you need to leave plenty of room for the mixture to spread during baking. Line the sheets with non-stick baking paper.

Scales and measuring spoons – these are necessary for accurate weighing and measuring.

Electric whisk – although not essential you'll save time and energy by using a stand or hand-held electric whisk for the first stages of making the whoopie pie batter and for making the fillings.

Flexible plastic spatula – a firm handled rubber or silicone spatula is ideal for scraping the batter down the sides of the bowl and making sure all the dry ingredients are thoroughly incorporated. It's also great to use when filling pastry bags with the cake batter or filling.

Pastry bag and tip – to get even-sized and round whoopie pies it's best to pipe the batter onto the baking sheets. A large capacity nylon, fabric or disposable plastic pastry bag fitted with a large plain piping tip will do the trick.

Large and small palette knives – use a large palette knife to transfer the whoopie pies to a wire rack. A small palette knife is perfect for spreading filling or frosting onto the baked whoopies.

INGREDIENTS FOR THE TASTIEST WHOOPIES

Butter – although many traditional recipes use vegetable shortening to make whoopie pies, most of the recipes in this book are made with butter or a mixture of butter and shortening which produces a richer flavour and a slightly firmer cake which is easier to fill. Use lightly salted butter and allow it to soften at room temperature before using. For buttercream use an unsalted butter.

Vegetable shortening – a soft flavourless fat which is creamed with butter to give lighter more crumbly textured cakes. If you prefer you can replace the butter with vegetable shortening.

Sugar – use caster sugar for pale or delicately flavoured whoopie pies such as lemon or vanilla.

Soft light brown and soft dark brown sugars are best for whoopie pies with stronger flavourings such as chocolate and ginger.

Eggs – remove from the fridge for 1 hour before using.

Flour and raising agents – plain or wholemeal flour is used to make whoopie pies with the addition of bicarbonate of soda or baking powder as the raising agent. Take care when measuring the raising agent as too much may cause the cakes to collapse when they come out of the oven.

Milk, sour cream and cultured buttermilk – the liquid element of the whoopie pie mixture, these acidic liquids help to create a chemical reaction with the raising agent to create light and airy cakes.

Vanilla extract – an essential flavouring in many of the whoopie pies. Make sure to buy the real thing for the best flavour.

TOP TIPS FOR MAKING WONDERFUL WHOOPIES

- If the creamed mixture begins to curdle a little when you add the egg, stir in a spoonful of the sieved flour mixture.
- Piping the whoopie pie batter onto the baking sheets will ensure fairly even-sized and shaped rounds but using a tablespoon or small ice cream scoop will work just as well. Try and keep the mounds as round as possible and don't be tempted to spread or flatten them.
- Remember oven temperatures can vary considerably. Fan ovens cook more quickly than conventional ovens, so reduce the temperature by 10–20°C/50–68°F. Check the whoopie pies after about 6–8 minutes.
- To check if the whoopie pies are cooked, lightly press the top of one with your fingertip – if the pie springs back it's ready, if it leaves a slight indentation then return to the oven for a further couple of minutes.

- Don't be tempted to transfer the whoopies pies to a wire rack as soon as they come out of the oven. They need at least 5 minutes to allow them to firm up and cool slightly.
- However neatly you piped or spooned the batter onto the baking sheets you will probably still find slight variations in the shapes and sizes of the baked whoopie pies. But it's not a problem - just match them up accordingly when pairing them together before filling.
- To fill a whoopie pie, pipe a large swirl or drop a heaped spoonful of the filling onto the centre of one cake. Place a second cake on top and press down gently. If the filling is a little soft, chill the filled pies in the refrigerator for 1–2 hours.
- To freeze unfilled whoopie pies, spread them on a baking sheet and open freeze until solid, then pack away in freezer boxes or bags interleaved with baking paper. To defrost, spread the frozen whoopie pies in a single layer on baking sheets and leave at room temperature for 1–2 hours.
- Filled whoopie pies are best eaten on the day of filling; however, they will keep for up to 2–3 days in an airtight container. Whoopie pies with a cream or cream cheese filling should be kept in the refrigerator, but remove them and leave at room temperature for 30 minutes before serving.
- Finally, don't be afraid to experiment – once you've enjoyed a few of these whoopie pie recipes why not try your own flavour variation or mix and match the different fillings and toppings? The variations are endless!
- Above all, have fun making whoopies!!!

Classic Whoopie

chocolate whoopie pies

makes 10

175 g/6 oz plain flour

1½ tsp bicarbonate of soda

40 g/1½ oz cocoa powder

large pinch of salt

85 g/3 oz butter, softened

85 g/3 oz white vegetable fat

150 g/5½ oz soft dark brown sugar

1 large egg, beaten

1 tsp vanilla extract

150 ml/5 fl oz milk

marshmallow filling

225 g/8 oz white marshmallows

4 tbsp milk

115 g/4 oz white vegetable fat

55 g/2 oz icing sugar, sifted

Preheat the oven to 180°C/350°F/Gas Mark 4. Line 2–3 large baking sheets with baking paper. Sift together the plain flour, bicarbonate of soda, cocoa powder and salt.

Place the butter, white vegetable fat and sugar in a large bowl and beat with an electric whisk until pale and fluffy. Beat in the egg and vanilla extract followed by half the flour mixture and then the milk. Stir in the rest of the flour mixture and mix until thoroughly incorporated.

Pipe or spoon 20 mounds of the mixture onto the prepared baking sheets, spaced well apart to allow for spreading. Bake in the preheated oven, one sheet at a time, for 12–14 minutes until risen and just firm to the touch. Cool for 5 minutes, then using a palette knife transfer to a wire rack and leave to cool completely.

For the filling, place the marshmallows and milk in a heatproof bowl set over a pan of simmering water. Leave until the marshmallows have melted, stirring occasionally. Remove from the heat and leave to cool.

Place the white vegetable fat and icing sugar in a bowl and beat together until smooth and creamy. Add the creamed mixture to the marshmallow and beat for 1–2 minutes until fluffy.

To assemble, spread the filling over the flat side of half the cakes. Top with the rest of the cakes.

vanilla whoopie pies

makes 12

250 g/9 oz plain flour

1 tsp bicarbonate of soda

large pinch of salt

175 g/6 oz butter, softened

150 g/5½ oz caster sugar

1 large egg, beaten

2 tsp vanilla extract

150 ml/5 fl oz buttermilk

chocolate buttercream filling

115 g/4 oz milk chocolate, broken into pieces

115 g/4 oz unsalted butter, softened

250 g/9 oz icing sugar, sifted

Preheat the oven to 180°C/350°F/Gas Mark 4. Line 2–3 large baking sheets with baking paper. Sift together the plain flour, bicarbonate of soda and salt.

Place the butter and sugar in a large bowl and beat with an electric whisk until pale and fluffy. Beat in the egg and vanilla extract followed by half the flour mixture and then the buttermilk. Stir in the rest of the flour mixture and mix until thoroughly incorporated.

Pipe or spoon 24 mounds of the mixture onto the prepared baking sheets, spaced well apart to allow for spreading. Bake in the preheated oven, one sheet at a time, for 10–12 minutes until risen and just firm to the touch. Cool for 5 minutes then using a palette knife transfer to a wire rack and leave to cool completely.

For the filling, place the chocolate in a heatproof bowl set over a pan of simmering water and leave until melted. Remove from the heat and leave to cool for 20 minutes, stirring occasionally. Place the butter in a bowl and beat with an electric whisk for 2–3 minutes until pale and creamy. Gradually beat in the icing sugar then beat in the chocolate.

To assemble, spread or pipe the buttercream on the flat side of half of the cakes. Top with the rest of the cakes.

red velvet whoopie pies

makes 10

200 g/7 oz plain flour

1½ tsp bicarbonate of soda

25 g/1 oz cocoa powder

large pinch of salt

85 g/3 oz butter, softened

85 g/3 oz white vegetable fat

150 g/5½ oz soft light brown sugar

1 large egg, beaten

1 tsp vanilla extract

1 tbsp red food colouring

150 ml/5 fl oz soured cream

vanilla filling

250 g/9 oz full-fat soft cheese, at room temperature

55 g/2 oz unsalted butter, softened

few drops vanilla extract

85 g/3 oz icing sugar, sifted

Preheat the oven to 180°C/350°F/Gas Mark 4. Line 2–3 large baking sheets with baking paper. Sift together the plain flour, bicarbonate of soda, cocoa powder and salt.

Place the butter, white vegetable fat and sugar in a large bowl and beat with an electric whisk until pale and fluffy. Beat in the egg, vanilla extract and food colouring followed by half the flour mixture and then the soured cream. Stir in the rest of the flour mixture and mix until thoroughly incorporated.

Pipe or spoon 20 mounds of the mixture onto the prepared baking sheets, spaced well apart to allow for spreading. Bake, one sheet at a time, in the preheated oven for 12–14 minutes until risen and just firm to the touch. Cool for 5 minutes then using a palette knife transfer to a wire rack and leave to cool completely.

For the filling, place the soft cheese and butter in a bowl and beat together until well blended. Beat in the vanilla extract and icing sugar until smooth.

To assemble, spread or pipe the filling over the flat side of half the cakes. Top with the rest of the cakes.

oatmeal & raisin whoopie pies

makes 12

250 g/9 oz plain flour

2 tsp baking powder

large pinch of salt

1 tsp ground mixed spice

115 g/4 oz butter, softened

150 g/5½ oz soft light brown sugar

1 large egg, beaten

150 ml/5 fl oz milk

85 g/3 oz rolled oats

55 g/2 oz raisins

orange buttercream filling

115 g/4 oz unsalted butter, softened

finely grated rind and juice from 1 orange

200 g/7 oz icing sugar

Preheat the oven to 180°C/350°F/Gas Mark 4. Line 2–3 large baking sheets with baking paper. Sift together the plain flour, baking powder, salt and mixed spice.

Place the butter and sugar in a large bowl and beat with an electric whisk until pale and fluffy. Whisk in the egg followed by half the flour mixture and then the milk. Stir in the rest of the flour mixture and mix until thoroughly incorporated. Stir in the rolled oats and raisins.

Pipe or spoon 24 mounds of the mixture onto the prepared baking sheets, spaced well apart to allow for spreading. Bake, one sheet at a time, in the preheated oven for 10–12 minutes until risen and just firm to the touch. Cool for 5 minutes then using a palette knife transfer to a wire rack and leave to cool completely.

For the filling, place the butter, orange rind and juice in a bowl and beat with an electric whisk for 2–3 minutes until pale and creamy. Gradually beat in the icing sugar and continue beating for 2–3 minutes until the buttercream is very light and fluffy.

To assemble, spread or pipe the buttercream on the flat side of half of the cakes. Top with the rest of the cakes.

pumpkin whoopie pies

makes 12

275 g/9¾ oz plain flour

½ tsp baking powder

½ tsp bicarbonate of soda

1½ tsp ground cinnamon

¼ tsp salt

200 g/7 oz light brown soft sugar

125 ml/4 fl oz sunflower oil

1 large egg, beaten

1 tsp vanilla extract

115 g/4 oz canned pumpkin purée

cinnamon & maple filling

200 g/7 oz full fat soft cheese

85 g/3 oz unsalted butter, softened

2 tbsp maple syrup

1 tsp ground cinnamon

85 g/3 oz icing sugar, sifted

Preheat the oven to 180°C/350°F/Gas Mark 4. Line 2–3 large baking sheets with baking paper. Sift together the plain flour, baking powder, bicarbonate of soda, cinnamon and salt.

Place the sugar and oil in a large bowl and beat with an electric whisk for 1 minute. Whisk in the egg and vanilla extract then the pumpkin purée. Stir in the sifted flour mixture and beat until thoroughly incorporated.

Pipe or spoon 24 mounds of the mixture onto the prepared baking sheets, spaced well apart to allow for spreading. Bake, one sheet at a time, in the preheated oven for 8–10 minutes until risen and just firm to the touch. Cool for 5 minutes then using a palette knife transfer to a cooling rack and leave to cool completely.

For the filling, place the soft cheese and butter in a bowl and beat together until well blended. Beat in the maple syrup, cinnamon and icing sugar until smooth.

To assemble, spread or pipe the filling over the flat side of half the cakes. Top with the rest of the cakes.

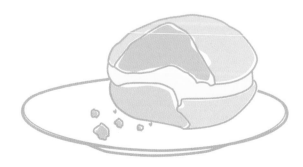

chocolate chip whoopie pies

makes 10

250 g/9 oz plain flour

1 tsp bicarbonate of soda

large pinch of salt

115 g/4 oz butter, softened

150 g/5½ oz soft light brown sugar

1 large egg, beaten

1 tsp vanilla extract

150 ml/5 fl oz soured cream

85 g/3 oz milk chocolate chips

chocolate filling

150 g/5½ oz plain chocolate, broken into pieces

115 g/4 oz unsalted butter, softened

150 ml/5 fl oz double cream

Preheat the oven to 180°C/350°F/Gas Mark 4. Line 2–3 large baking sheets with baking paper. Sift together the plain flour, bicarbonate of soda and salt.

Place the butter and sugar in a large bowl and beat with an electric whisk until pale and fluffy. Whisk in the egg and vanilla extract, followed by half the flour mixture and then the soured cream. Stir in the rest of the flour mixture and mix until thoroughly incorporated. Stir in half the chocolate chips

Pipe or spoon 20 mounds of the mixture onto the prepared baking sheets, spaced well apart to allow for spreading. Sprinkle over the rest of the chocolate chips. Bake in the preheated oven, one sheet at a time, for 10–12 minutes until risen and just firm to the touch. Cool for 5 minutes then using a palette knife transfer to a wire rack and leave to cool completely.

For the filling, place the chocolate and butter in a heatproof bowl set over a pan of simmering water and leave until melted, stirring occasionally. Remove from the heat and leave to cool for 20 minutes. Stir the cream into the cooled chocolate then chill in the refrigerator for 10–15 minutes until firm enough to spread.

To assemble, spread or pipe the chocolate filling on the flat side of half of the cakes. Top with the rest of the cakes.

gingerbread whoopie pies

makes 10

200 g/7 oz plain flour

1½ tsp bicarbonate of soda

2 tsp ground ginger

¼ tsp salt

85 g/3 oz butter, softened

85 g/3 oz white vegetable fat

115 g/4 oz soft dark brown sugar

2 tbsp black treacle

1 large egg, beaten

100 ml/3½ fl oz milk

ginger cream filling

225 g/8 oz full fat soft cheese

115 g/4 oz icing sugar, sifted

4 tbsp double cream

2 pieces stem ginger, finely chopped

Preheat the oven to 180°C/350°F/Gas Mark 4. Line 2–3 large baking sheets with baking paper. Sift together the plain flour, bicarbonate of soda, ginger and salt.

Place the butter, white vegetable fat and sugar in a large bowl and beat with an electric whisk until pale and fluffy. Whisk in the black treacle and egg followed by half the flour mixture and then the milk. Stir in the rest of the flour mixture and mix until thoroughly incorporated.

Pipe or spoon 20 mounds of the mixture onto the prepared baking sheets, spaced well apart to allow for spreading. Bake, one sheet at a time, in the preheated oven for 11–13 minutes until risen and just firm to the touch. Cool for 5 minutes then using a palette knife transfer to a wire rack and leave to cool completely.

For the filling, place the soft cheese, icing sugar and cream in a bowl and using an electric whisk, beat together briefly until just smooth. Stir in the stem ginger.

To assemble, spread or pipe the filling over the flat side of half the cakes. Top with the rest of the cakes.

peanut butter & jam whoopie pies

makes 14

250 g/9 oz plain flour

1 tsp bicarbonate of soda

large pinch of salt

115 g/4 oz butter, softened

150 g/5½ oz light muscovado sugar

1 large egg, beaten

150 ml/5 fl oz buttermilk

85 g/3 oz unsalted peanuts, finely ground

1 tbsp salted peanuts, roughly chopped

3 tbsp seedless raspberry jam

peanut butter buttercream filling

115 g/4 oz unsalted butter, softened

115 g/4 oz crunchy peanut butter

140 g/5 oz icing sugar, sifted

Preheat the oven to 180°C/350°F/Gas Mark 4. Line 2–3 large baking sheets with baking paper. Sift together the plain flour, bicarbonate of soda and salt.

Place the butter and sugar in a large bowl and beat with an electric whisk until pale and fluffy. Beat in the egg, followed by half the flour mixture and then the buttermilk. Stir in the rest of the flour mixture and mix until thoroughly incorporated. Fold in the unsalted ground peanuts.

Pipe or spoon 28 mounds of the mixture onto the prepared baking sheets, spaced well apart to allow for spreading. Sprinkle with the chopped salted nuts. Bake in the preheated oven, one sheet at a time, for 10–12 minutes until risen and just firm to the touch. Cool for 5 minutes then using a palette knife transfer to a wire rack and leave to cool completely.

For the filling, place the butter and peanut butter in a bowl and beat with an electric whisk for 5 minutes until pale and fluffy. Gradually beat in the icing sugar until smooth.

To assemble, spread or pipe the buttercream on the flat side of half of the cakes and top with a thin layer of jam. Top with the rest of the cakes.

Well-dressed Whoopie

banana maple cream whoopie pies

makes 12

250 g/9 oz plain flour

1 tsp bicarbonate of soda

large pinch of salt

115 g/4 oz butter, softened

150 g/5½ oz light muscovado sugar

1 large egg, beaten

6 tbsp buttermilk

1 large ripe banana, peeled and mashed

85 g/3 oz pecan nuts, finely chopped

maple cream filling

300 ml/10 fl oz double cream

3 tbsp maple syrup

Preheat the oven to 180°C/350°F/Gas Mark 4. Line 2–3 large baking sheets with baking paper. Sift together the plain flour, bicarbonate of soda and salt.

Place the butter and sugar in a large bowl and beat with an electric whisk until pale and fluffy. Beat in the egg followed by half the flour mixture then the buttermilk. Stir in the rest of the flour mixture and mix until thoroughly incorporated. Stir in the mashed banana.

Pipe or spoon 24 mounds of the mixture onto the prepared baking sheets, spaced well apart to allow for spreading. Bake in the preheated oven, one sheet at a time, for 10–12 minutes until risen and just firm to the touch. Cool for 5 minutes then using a palette knife transfer to a wire rack and leave to cool completely.

For the filling, place the cream and maple syrup in a bowl and whip together until holding firm peaks.

To assemble, spread or pipe the maple cream on the flat side of half of the cakes. Top with the rest of the cakes. Spread the chopped pecans on a plate and gently roll the edges of each whoopie pie in the nuts to lightly coat.

luscious lemon whoopie pies

makes 10

250 g/9 oz plain flour

2 tsp baking powder

large pinch of salt

115 g/4 oz butter, softened

150 g/5½ oz caster sugar

finely grated rind of 1 lemon

1 large egg, beaten

100 ml/3½ fl oz milk

4 tbsp lemon curd

1 tbsp yellow sugar sprinkles,
to decorate

lemon buttercream filling

115 g/4 oz unsalted butter,
softened

2 tbsp lemon juice

200 g/7 oz icing sugar, sifted

icing

115 g/4 oz icing sugar

1–2 tbsp warm water

Preheat the oven to 180°C/350°F/Gas Mark 4. Line 2–3 large baking sheets with baking paper. Sift together the plain flour, baking powder and salt.

Place the butter, sugar and lemon rind in a large bowl and beat with an electric whisk until pale and fluffy. Beat in the egg followed by half the flour mixture then the milk. Stir in the rest of the flour mixture and mix until thoroughly incorporated.

Pipe or spoon 20 mounds of the mixture onto the prepared baking sheets, spaced well apart to allow for spreading. Bake in the preheated oven, one sheet at a time, for 10–12 minutes until risen and just firm to the touch. Cool for 5 minutes then using a palette knife transfer to a wire rack and leave to cool completely.

For the filling, place the butter and lemon juice in a bowl and beat with an electric whisk for 2–3 minutes until pale and creamy. Gradually beat in the icing sugar and continue beating for 2–3 minutes until the buttercream is very light and fluffy.

For the icing, sift the icing sugar into a bowl and gradually stir in enough water to make a smooth icing that is thick enough to coat the back of a wooden spoon.

To assemble, spread or pipe the buttercream on the flat side of half of the cakes and the lemon curd over the other half of the cakes. Sandwich the cakes together. Spoon the icing over the whoopie pies and decorate with the sugar sprinkles.

coconut & raspberry mallow whoopie pies

makes 12

225 g/8 oz plain flour

2 tsp baking powder

large pinch of salt

115 g/4 oz desiccated coconut

115 g/4 oz butter, softened

150 g/5½ oz caster sugar

1 large egg, beaten

100 ml/3½ fl oz milk

3 tbsp raspberry jam

coconut mallow filling

115 g/4 oz white marshmallows

3 tbsp coconut milk

200 ml/7 fl oz double cream

Preheat the oven to 180°C/350°F/Gas Mark 4. Line 2–3 large baking sheets with baking paper. Sift together the plain flour, baking powder and salt. Stir in half the coconut. Lightly toast the rest of the coconut and set aside.

Place the butter and sugar in a large bowl and beat with an electric whisk until pale and fluffy. Beat in the egg followed by half the flour mixture then the milk. Stir in the rest of the flour mixture and mix until thoroughly incorporated.

Pipe or spoon 24 mounds of the mixture onto the prepared baking sheets, spaced well apart to allow for spreading. Bake in the preheated oven, one sheet at a time, for 10–12 minutes until risen and just firm to the touch. Cool for 5 minutes then using a palette knife transfer to a wire rack and leave to cool completely.

For the filling, place the marshmallows and coconut milk in a heatproof bowl set over a pan of simmering water. Leave until the marshmallows have melted, stirring occasionally. Remove from the heat and leave to cool. Whip the cream until holding firm peaks then fold into the marshmallow mixture. Cover and chill in the refrigerator until firm enough to spread.

To assemble, spread a thin layer of jam over the flat side of all the cakes. Place a spoonful of the coconut filling on half the cakes. Top with the rest of the cakes. Spread the toasted coconut on a plate and gently roll the edges of each whoopie pie in the coconut to lightly coat.

'be my valentine' whoopie pies

makes 14

250 g/9 oz plain flour

1 tsp bicarbonate of soda

large pinch of salt

115 g/4 oz butter, softened

150 g/5½ oz caster sugar

1 large egg, beaten

1 tsp vanilla extract

150 ml/5 fl oz buttermilk

¼ tsp red liquid food colouring

2 tbsp pink heart shaped sugar sprinkles

vanilla buttercream filling

150 g/5½ oz unsalted butter, softened

1 tsp vanilla extract

4 tbsp double cream

280 g/10 oz icing sugar, sifted

icing

150 g/5½ oz icing sugar

1–2 tbsp warm water

few drops red liquid food colouring

Preheat the oven to 180°C/350°F/Gas Mark 4. Line 2–3 large baking sheets with baking paper. Sift together the plain flour, bicarbonate of soda and salt.

Place the butter and sugar in a large bowl and beat with an electric whisk until pale and fluffy. Beat in the egg and vanilla extract followed by half the flour mixture then the buttermilk and food colouring. Stir in the rest of the flour mixture and mix until thoroughly incorporated.

Pipe or spoon 28 mounds of the mixture onto the prepared baking sheets, spaced well apart to allow for spreading. Bake in the preheated oven, one sheet at a time, for 9–11 minutes until risen and just firm to the touch. Cool for 5 minutes then using a palette knife transfer to a wire rack and leave to cool completely.

For the filling, place the butter and vanilla extract in a bowl and beat with an electric whisk for 2–3 minutes until pale and creamy. Beat in the cream then gradually beat in the icing sugar and continue beating for 2–3 minutes.

For the icing, sift the icing sugar into a bowl and stir in enough water to make a smooth icing that is thick enough to coat the back of a wooden spoon. Beat in a few drops of food colouring to colour the icing pale pink.

To assemble, spread or pipe the buttercream on the flat side of half of the cakes. Top with the rest of the cakes. Spoon the icing over the whoopie pies and decorate with the heart shaped sugar sprinkles. Leave to set.

double chocolate whoopie pies

makes 12

200 g/7 oz plain flour

1½ tsp bicarbonate of soda

25 g/1 oz cocoa powder

large pinch of salt

85 g/3 oz butter, softened

85 g/3 oz white vegetable fat

150 g/5½ oz soft light brown sugar

25 g/1 oz plain chocolate, finely grated

1 large egg, beaten

125 ml/4 fl oz milk

4 tbsp plain chocolate strands

white chocolate filling

175 g/6 oz white chocolate, broken into pieces

2 tbsp milk

300 ml/10 fl oz double cream

Preheat the oven to 180°C/350°F/Gas Mark 4. Line 2–3 large baking sheets with baking paper. Sift together the plain flour, bicarbonate of soda, cocoa powder and salt.

Place the butter, white vegetable fat, sugar and grated chocolate in a large bowl and beat with an electric whisk until pale and fluffy. Beat in the egg followed by half the flour mixture then the milk. Stir in the rest of the flour mixture and mix until thoroughly incorporated.

Pipe or spoon 24 mounds of the mixture onto the prepared baking sheets, spaced well apart to allow for spreading. Bake in the preheated oven, one sheet at a time, for 10–12 minutes until risen and just firm to the touch. Cool for 5 minutes then using a palette knife transfer to a wire rack and leave to cool completely.

For the filling, place the chocolate and milk in a heatproof bowl set over a pan of simmering water. Leave until the chocolate has melted, stirring occasionally. Remove from the heat and leave to cool for 30 minutes. Using an electric whisk, whip the cream until holding firm peaks. Fold in the chocolate. Cover and chill in the refrigerator for 30–45 minutes until firm enough to spread.

To assemble, spread or pipe the chocolate filling on the flat side of half the cakes. Top with the rest of the cakes. Spread the chocolate strands on a plate and gently roll the edges of each whoopie pie in the strands to lightly coat.

caramel fudge whoopie pies

makes 10

250 g/9 oz plain flour

2 tsp baking powder

large pinch of salt

115 g/4 oz butter, softened

85 g/3 oz soft dark brown sugar

2 tbsp golden syrup

1 large egg, beaten

1 tsp vanilla extract

125 ml/4 fl oz milk

25 g/1 oz fudge, finely chopped

caramel buttercream

125 g/4½ oz unsalted butter, softened

115 g/4 oz icing sugar

5 tbsp dulce de leche (caramel)

Preheat the oven to 180°C/350°F/Gas Mark 4. Line 2–3 large baking sheets with baking paper. Sift together the plain flour, baking powder and salt.

Place the butter and sugar in a large bowl and beat with an electric whisk until pale and fluffy. Beat in the golden syrup, egg and vanilla extract followed by half the flour mixture then the milk. Stir in the rest of the flour mixture and mix until thoroughly incorporated.

Pipe or spoon 20 mounds of the mixture onto the prepared baking sheets, spaced well apart to allow for spreading. Bake, one sheet at a time, in the preheated oven for 10–12 minutes until risen and just firm to the touch. Cool for 5 minutes then using a palette knife transfer to a wire rack and leave to cool completely.

For the filling, place the butter in a bowl and beat with an electric whisk for 2–3 minutes until pale and creamy. Gradually beat in the icing sugar and continue beating for 2–3 minutes until the buttercream is very light and fluffy. Stir in the dulce de leche.

To assemble, spread or pipe two thirds of the buttercream on the flat side of half of the cakes. Thinly spread the rest of the buttercream on the tops of the remaining cakes. Sandwich the cakes together and decorate with the chopped fudge.

chocolate & lime whoopie pies

makes 10

250 g/9 oz plain flour

1 tsp bicarbonate of soda

25 g/1 oz cocoa powder

large pinch of salt

115 g/4 oz butter, softened

150 g/5½ oz caster sugar

1 large egg, beaten

1 tsp vanilla extract

4 tbsp soured cream

3 tbsp milk

chocolate glaze

85 g/3 oz plain chocolate, broken into pieces

55 g/ 2 oz unsalted butter

lime soft cheese filling

175 g/6 oz full-fat soft cheese

85 g/3 oz unsalted butter, softened

juice and finely grated rind of 1 lime

115 g/4 oz icing sugar, sifted

Preheat the oven to 180°C/350°F/Gas Mark 4. Line 2–3 large baking sheets with baking paper. Sift together the plain flour, bicarbonate of soda, cocoa powder and salt.

Place the butter and sugar in a large bowl and beat with an electric whisk until pale and fluffy. Whisk in the egg and vanilla extract followed by half the flour mixture then the soured cream and milk. Stir in the rest of the flour mixture and mix until thoroughly incorporated.

Pipe or spoon 20 mounds of the mixture onto the prepared baking sheets, spaced well apart to allow for spreading. Bake in the preheated oven, one sheet at a time, for 10–12 minutes until risen and just firm to the touch. Cool for 5 minutes then using a palette knife transfer to a wire rack and leave to cool completely.

For the glaze, place the chocolate and butter in a heatproof bowl set over a pan of simmering water and leave until melted, stirring occasionally. Remove from the heat and leave to cool for 20 minutes, stirring occasionally.

For the filling, place the soft cheese, butter and lime juice and rind in a bowl and beat with an electric whisk until smooth. Gradually beat in the icing sugar.

To assemble, spread or pipe the lime filling on the flat side of half the cakes. Top with the rest of the cakes. Gently dip one half of each whoopie pie in the chocolate glaze and place on a cooling rack set over a baking sheet. Place in the refrigerator for 20 minutes until the glaze has just set.

malted milk whoopie pies

makes 25

225 g/8 oz plain flour

1 tsp bicarbonate of soda

large pinch of salt

55 g/2 oz malted milk powder

115 g/4 oz butter, softened

115 g/ 4 oz caster sugar

40 g/1½ oz soft light brown sugar

1 large egg, beaten

4 tbsp soured cream

3 tbsp milk

3 tbsp mini coloured chocolate
beans, to decorate

vanilla buttercream filling

150 g/5½ oz unsalted butter,
softened

1 tsp vanilla extract

5 tbsp double cream

280 g/10 oz icing sugar, sifted

icing

175 g/6 oz icing sugar

2–3 tbsp warm water

red, green and yellow liquid food
colouring

Preheat the oven to 180°C/350°F/Gas Mark 4. Line 2–3 large baking sheets with baking paper. Sift together the plain flour, bicarbonate of soda and salt. Stir in the malted milk powder.

Place the butter and sugars in a large bowl and beat with an electric whisk until pale and fluffy. Beat in the egg followed by half the flour mixture then the soured cream and milk. Stir in the rest of the flour mixture and beat until thoroughly incorporated.

Pipe or spoon 50 small mounds of the mixture onto the prepared baking sheets, spaced well apart to allow for spreading. Bake in the preheated oven, one sheet at a time, for 8–10 minutes until risen and just firm to the touch. Cool for 5 minutes then using a palette knife transfer to a wire rack and leave to cool completely.

For the filling, place the butter and vanilla extract in a bowl and beat with an electric whisk for 2–3 minutes until pale and creamy. Beat in the cream then gradually beat in the icing sugar and continue beating for 2–3 minutes until the buttercream is very light and fluffy.

For the icing, sift the icing sugar into a bowl and stir in and enough water together to make a smooth icing that is thick enough to coat the back of a wooden spoon. Divide the icing between three small bowls and beat in a few drops of red, green or yellow colouring to each bowl.

To assemble, spread or pipe the buttercream on the flat side of half of the cakes. Top with the rest of the cakes. Spoon the icings over the whoopie pies and decorate with the coloured chocolate beans. Leave to set.

Gourmet Whoopie

marbled mocha whoopie pies

makes 10

250 g/9 oz plain flour

1 tsp bicarbonate of soda

large pinch of salt

115 g/4 oz butter, softened

150 g/5½ oz caster sugar

1 large egg, beaten

150 ml/5 fl oz buttermilk

1 tsp vanilla extract

1 tsp cold strong black coffee or coffee extract

1 tbsp cocoa powder

chocolate & cream filling

140 g/5 oz plain chocolate, finely chopped

450 ml/16 fl oz double cream

1 tbsp cold strong black coffee

Preheat the oven to 180°C/350°F/Gas Mark 4. Line 2–3 large baking sheets with baking paper. Sift together the plain flour, bicarbonate of soda and salt.

Place the butter and sugar in a large bowl and beat with an electric whisk until pale and fluffy. Beat in the egg followed by half the flour mixture and then the buttermilk. Stir in the rest of the flour mixture, reserving 1 tbsp, and mix until thoroughly incorporated.

Transfer half the mixture to a second bowl. Stir the vanilla extract and remaining tbsp of flour mixture into one bowl. Stir the coffee or coffee extract and cocoa powder into the second bowl. Gently swirl the two mixtures together to create a marbled effect.

Pipe or spoon 20 mounds of the mixture onto the prepared baking sheets, spaced well apart to allow for spreading. Bake in the preheated oven, one sheet at a time, for 10–12 minutes until risen and just firm to the touch. Cool for 5 minutes then using a palette knife transfer to a wire rack and leave to cool completely.

For the filling, place the chocolate in a heatproof bowl. Heat 200 ml/7 fl oz of the cream and the coffee in a small heavy-based saucepan until boiling then pour over the chocolate and stir until the chocolate has melted. Leave to cool for 20–30 minutes, stirring occasionally, until thickened. Whip the rest of the cream until holding firm peaks.

To assemble, spread or pipe the chocolate mixture on the flat side of half of the cakes and top with the whipped cream. Top with the rest of the cakes.

black forest whoopie pies

makes 10

250 g/9 oz plain flour

1 tsp bicarbonate of soda

25 g/1 oz cocoa powder

large pinch of salt

115 g/4 oz butter, softened

150 g/5½ oz soft dark brown sugar

1 large egg, beaten

1 tsp vanilla extract

4 tbsp soured cream

3 tbsp milk

55 g/2 oz dried and sweetened sour cherries, chopped

cocoa powder, to dust

filling

300 ml/10 fl oz double cream

2 tbsp cherry liqueur (optional)

6 tbsp cherry conserve

55 g/2 oz plain chocolate, grated

Preheat the oven to 180°C/350°F/Gas Mark 4. Line 2–3 large baking sheets with baking paper. Sift together the plain flour, bicarbonate of soda, cocoa powder and salt.

Place the butter and sugar in a large bowl and beat with an electric whisk until pale and fluffy. Whisk in the egg and vanilla extract followed by half the flour mixture then the soured cream and milk. Stir in the rest of the flour mixture and mix until thoroughly incorporated. Stir in the chopped dried cherries.

Pipe or spoon 20 mounds of the mixture onto the prepared baking sheets, spaced well apart to allow for spreading. Bake in the preheated oven, one sheet at a time, for 10–12 minutes until risen and just firm to the touch. Cool for 5 minutes then using a palette knife transfer to a wire rack and leave to cool completely.

For the filling, place the cream and cherry liqueur (if using) in a bowl and whip until holding firm peaks.

To assemble, spread the cherry conserve on the flat side of half the cakes. Top with the whipped cream and the grated chocolate. Top with the rest of the cakes. Dust lightly with cocoa powder.

pistachio & honey whoopie pies

makes 12

250 g/9 oz plain flour

1 tsp bicarbonate of soda

large pinch of salt

70 g/2½ oz pistachio nuts, finely ground, plus 1 tbsp chopped

115 g/4 oz butter, softened

150 g/5½ oz caster sugar

finely grated rind of ½ lemon

1 large egg, beaten

150 ml/5 fl oz buttermilk

honey mascarpone filling

250 g/9 oz mascarpone cheese

125 ml/4 fl oz double cream

4 tbsp dark runny honey

Preheat the oven to 180°C/350°F/Gas Mark 4. Line 2–3 large baking sheets with baking paper. Sift together the plain flour, bicarbonate of soda and salt. Stir in the ground pistachio nuts.

Place the butter, sugar and lemon rind in a large bowl and beat with an electric whisk until pale and fluffy. Beat in the egg, followed by half the flour mixture and then the buttermilk. Stir in the rest of the flour mixture and mix until thoroughly incorporated.

Pipe or spoon 24 mounds of the mixture onto the prepared baking sheets, spaced well apart to allow for spreading. Sprinkle with the chopped pistachio nuts. Bake in the preheated oven, one sheet at a time, for 10–12 minutes until risen and just firm to the touch. Cool for 5 minutes then using a palette knife transfer to a wire rack and leave to cool completely.

For the filling, place the mascarpone and cream in a bowl and beat until smooth. Stir in the honey and chill in the refrigerator for 30 minutes.

To assemble, spread or pipe the mascarpone cream on the flat side of half of the cakes. Top with the rest of the cakes.

strawberry & cream whoopie pies

makes 12

250 g/9 oz plain flour

1 tsp bicarbonate of soda

large pinch of salt

115 g/4 oz butter, softened

150 g/5½ oz caster sugar

1 large egg, beaten

2 tsp rosewater

150 ml/5 fl oz buttermilk

icing sugar, to dust

filling

300 ml/10 fl oz double cream

4 tbsp icing sugar, sifted

3 tbsp strawberry conserve

225 g/8 oz strawberries, hulled
and sliced

Preheat the oven to 180°C/350°F/Gas Mark 4. Line 2–3 large baking sheets with baking paper. Sift together the plain flour, bicarbonate of soda and salt.

Place the butter and sugar in a large bowl and beat with an electric whisk until pale and fluffy. Beat in the egg and rosewater followed by half the flour mixture and then the buttermilk. Stir in the rest of the flour mixture and mix until thoroughly incorporated.

Pipe or spoon 24 mounds of the mixture onto the prepared baking sheets, spaced well apart to allow for spreading. Bake in the preheated oven, one sheet at a time, for 10–12 minutes until risen and just firm to the touch. Cool for 5 minutes then using a palette knife transfer to a wire rack and leave to cool completely.

For the filling, place the cream in a bowl and whip until holding firm peaks. Fold in the sifted icing sugar.

To assemble, spread the strawberry conserve on the flat side of half of the cakes followed by the whipped cream and strawberries. Top with the rest of the cakes. Dust with icing sugar.

spiced carrot & orange whoopie pies

makes 10

250 g/9 oz wholemeal flour

2 tsp baking powder

large pinch of salt

1½ tsp ground mixed spice

55 g/2 oz butter, softened

55 g/2 oz white vegetable fat

150 g/5½ oz soft light brown sugar

1 large egg, beaten

100 ml/3½ fl oz milk

140 g/5 oz carrots, peeled and finely grated

25 g/1 oz walnuts, chopped

115 g/4 oz ready-to-roll fondant icing

orange and green food colouring paste

orange filling

225 g/8 oz full-fat soft cheese

115 g/4 oz unsalted butter, softened

finely grated rind and 2 tbsp juice from 1 orange

200 g/7 oz icing sugar

1 tsp ground mixed spice

Preheat the oven to 180°C/350°F/Gas Mark 4. Line 2–3 large baking sheets with baking paper. Sift together the wholemeal flour, baking powder, salt and mixed spice, tipping any bran left in the sieve into the bowl.

Place the butter, white vegetable fat and sugar in a large bowl and beat with an electric whisk until pale and fluffy. Whisk in the egg followed by half the flour mixture and then the milk. Stir in the rest of the flour mixture and mix until thoroughly incorporated. Stir in the carrots and walnuts.

Pipe or spoon 20 mounds of the mixture onto the prepared baking sheets, spaced well apart to allow for spreading. Bake in the preheated oven, one sheet at a time, for 10–12 minutes until risen and just firm to the touch. Cool for 5 minutes then using a palette knife transfer to a wire rack and leave to cool completely.

For the filling, place the soft cheese, butter, orange rind and juice in a bowl and beat with an electric whisk for 2–3 minutes until pale and creamy. Gradually beat in the icing sugar and ground mixed spice until smooth.

To assemble, spread or pipe the orange filling on the flat side of half of the cakes. Top with the rest of the cakes. Colour three-quarters of the fondant icing orange and the rest green and shape into 10 mini carrots with leaves. Place one on top of each whoopie pie.

hazelnut praline whoopie pies

makes 10

250 g/9 oz plain flour

1 tsp bicarbonate of soda

large pinch of salt

115 g/4 oz butter, softened

150 g/5½ oz soft dark brown sugar

1 large egg, beaten

150 ml/5 fl oz buttermilk

55 g/2 oz chopped hazelnuts, lightly toasted

praline buttercream filling

140 g/5 oz caster sugar

40 g/1½ oz chopped hazelnuts

175 g/6 oz unsalted butter, softened

175 g/6 oz icing sugar, sifted

4 tbsp double cream

Preheat the oven to 180°C/350°F/Gas Mark 4. Line 2–3 large baking sheets with baking paper. Sift together the plain flour, bicarbonate of soda and salt.

Place the butter and sugar in a large bowl and beat with an electric whisk until pale and fluffy. Beat in the egg, followed by half the flour mixture and then the buttermilk. Stir in the rest of the flour mixture and mix until thoroughly incorporated. Fold in the chopped hazelnuts.

Pipe or spoon 20 mounds of the mixture onto the prepared baking sheets, spaced well apart to allow for spreading. Bake in the preheated oven, one sheet at a time, for 10–12 minutes until risen and just firm to the touch. Cool for 5 minutes then using a palette knife transfer to a wire rack and leave to cool completely.

For the filling, place the sugar in a heavy-based saucepan and heat gently until dissolved. Continue cooking, without stirring and occasionally swirling the pan, until the liquid has turned to a deep golden caramel. Spread the chopped hazelnuts on a non-stick baking sheet and quickly pour the hot caramel over the nuts. Leave until cold and set. Break the praline into smaller pieces and crush with a toffee hammer or in a food processor.

Place the butter in a bowl and beat with an electric whisk for 2–3 minutes until pale and creamy. Gradually beat in the icing sugar and cream and beat for 2–3 minutes. Stir in two-thirds of the crushed praline.

To assemble, spread or pipe the buttercream on the flat side of half of the cakes. Top with the rest of the cakes. Spread the remaining praline on a plate and gently roll the edges of each whoopie pie in the praline to coat.

after dinner mint whoopie pies

makes 30

175 g/6 oz plain flour

1½ tsp bicarbonate of soda

40 g/1½ oz cocoa powder

large pinch of salt

85 g/3 oz butter, softened

85 g/3 oz white vegetable fat

150 g/5½ oz soft light brown sugar

1 large egg, beaten

150 ml/5 fl oz milk

Icing sugar, for dusting

mint filling

300 g/10½ oz full-fat soft cheese

150 g/5½ oz unsalted butter, softened

1 tsp of peppermint extract

280 g/10 oz icing sugar, sifted

few drops green food colouring

Preheat the oven to 180°C/350°F/Gas Mark 4. Line 2–3 large baking sheets with baking paper. Sift together the plain flour, bicarbonate of soda, cocoa powder and salt.

Place the butter, white vegetable fat and sugar in a large bowl and beat with an electric whisk until pale and fluffy. Beat in the egg followed by half the flour mixture and then the milk. Stir in the rest of the flour mixture and mix until thoroughly incorporated.

Pipe or spoon 60 small mounds of the mixture onto the prepared baking sheets, spaced well apart to allow for spreading. Bake in the preheated oven, one sheet at a time, for 8–10 minutes until risen and just firm to the touch. Cool for 5 minutes then using a palette knife transfer to a wire rack and leave to cool completely.

For the filling, place the soft cheese and butter in a bowl and beat together until well blended. Beat in the peppermint extract and icing sugar until smooth. Transfer half the mixture to a second bowl and stir in a few drops of food colouring to give a pale green colour. Chill both fillings in the refrigerator for 30 minutes.

To assemble, carefully spoon the two fillings alternately into a piping bag fitted with a star-shaped nozzle. Pipe swirls of the filling onto the flat side of half the cakes. Top with the rest of the cakes.

snickerdoodle whoopie pies

makes 15

250 g/9 oz plain flour

1 tsp bicarbonate of soda

large pinch of salt

2 tsp ground cinnamon

115 g/4 oz butter, softened

150 g/5½ oz caster sugar plus 2 tbsp

1 large egg, beaten

1 tsp vanilla extract

150 ml/5 fl oz buttermilk

coffee filling

115 g/4 oz unsalted butter, softened

85 g/3 oz full-fat soft cheese

1 tbsp strong cold black coffee

280 g/10 oz icing sugar, sifted

Preheat the oven to 180°C/350°F/Gas Mark 4. Line 2–3 large baking sheets with baking paper. Sift together the plain flour, bicarbonate of soda, salt and 1 teaspoon of the cinnamon.

Place the butter and the 150 g/5½ oz, caster sugar in a large bowl and beat with an electric whisk until pale and fluffy. Beat in the egg and vanilla extract followed by half the flour mixture and then the buttermilk. Stir in the rest of the flour mixture and mix until thoroughly incorporated.

Pipe or spoon 30 mounds of the mixture onto the prepared baking sheets, spaced well apart to allow for spreading. Mix together the rest of the cinnamon with the 2 tbsp of caster sugar and sprinkle liberally over the mounds. Bake in the preheated oven, one sheet at a time, for 10–12 minutes until risen and just firm to the touch. Cool for 5 minutes then using a palette knife transfer to a wire rack and leave to cool completely.

For the filling, place the butter, soft cheese and coffee in a bowl and beat together until well blended. Gradually beat in the icing sugar until smooth.

To assemble, spread or pipe the coffee filling on the flat side of half of the cakes. Top with the rest of the cakes.

Party Whoopie

tutti frutti whoopie pies

makes 25

250 g/9 oz plain flour

1 tsp bicarbonate of soda

large pinch of salt

115 g/4 oz butter, softened

150 g/5½ oz caster sugar

1 large egg, beaten

½ tsp vanilla extract

150 ml/5 fl oz buttermilk

115 g/4 oz mixed coloured glacé cherries, finely chopped

4 tbsp multi-coloured sugar sprinkles

marshmallow filling

225 g/8 oz white marshmallows

4 tbsp milk

few drops red food colouring

115 g/4 oz white vegetable fat

55 g/2 oz icing sugar, sifted

Preheat the oven to 180°C/350°F/Gas Mark 4. Line 2–3 large baking sheets with baking paper. Sift together the plain flour, bicarbonate of soda and salt.

Place the butter and sugar in a large bowl and beat with an electric whisk until pale and fluffy. Beat in the egg and vanilla extract followed by half the flour mixture and then the buttermilk. Stir in the rest of the flour mixture and mix until thoroughly incorporated. Stir in the chopped cherries.

Pipe or spoon 50 small mounds of the mixture onto the prepared baking sheets, spaced well apart to allow for spreading. Bake in the preheated oven, one sheet at a time, for 9–11 minutes until risen and just firm to the touch. Cool for 5 minutes then using a palette knife transfer to a wire rack and leave to cool completely.

For the filling, place the marshmallows, milk and food colouring in a heatproof bowl set over a pan of simmering water. Leave until the marshmallows have melted, stirring occasionally. Remove from the heat and leave to cool.

Place the white vegetable fat and icing sugar in a bowl and beat together until smooth and creamy. Add the creamed mixture to the marshmallow and beat for 1–2 minutes until fluffy.

To assemble, spread the filling over the flat side of half of the cakes. Top with the remaining cakes. Spread the sugar sprinkles on a plate and gently roll the edges of each whoopie pie in the sprinkles to lightly coat.

toffee nut ice cream whoopie pies

makes 12

250 g/9 oz plain flour

1 tsp bicarbonate of soda

1 tsp ground mixed spice

large pinch of salt

115 g/4 oz butter, softened

150 g/5½ oz soft light brown sugar

1 large egg, beaten

4 tbsp soured cream

3 tbsp milk

55 g/2 oz chopped mixed nuts

filling

425 ml/15 fl oz vanilla ice cream

8 tbsp dulce de leche (caramel)

Preheat the oven to 180°C/350°F/Gas Mark 4. Line 2–3 large baking sheets with baking paper. Sift together the plain flour, bicarbonate of soda, mixed spice and salt.

Place the butter and sugar in a large bowl and beat with an electric whisk until pale and fluffy. Whisk in the egg followed by half the flour mixture then the soured cream and milk. Stir in the rest of the flour mixture and mix until thoroughly incorporated. Stir in the nuts.

Pipe or spoon 24 mounds of the mixture onto the prepared baking sheets, spaced well apart to allow for spreading. Bake in the preheated oven, one sheet at a time, for 10–12 minutes until risen and just firm to the touch. Cool for 5 minutes then using a palette knife transfer to a wire rack and leave to cool completely.

To assemble, remove the ice cream from the freezer and leave to soften for 15 minutes. Spread a layer of dulce de leche on half the cakes and top with a generous scoop of ice cream. Top with the rest of the cakes, pressing down gently. Serve immediately or wrap the whoopie pies individually in cling film and freeze. Remove from the freezer 30 minutes before serving.

chocolate whoopie pie birthday cake

serves 8

175 g/6 oz plain flour

1½ tsp bicarbonate of soda

40 g/1½ oz cocoa powder

large pinch of salt

85 g/3 oz butter, softened

85 g/3 oz white vegetable fat

150 g/5½ oz soft dark brown sugar

1 large egg, beaten

1 tsp vanilla extract

150 ml/5 fl oz milk

6 tbsp strawberry jam

icing sugar, to dust

birthday candles, to decorate

marshmallow filling

175 g/6 oz white marshmallows

3 tbsp milk

200 ml/7 fl oz double cream

Preheat the oven to 180°C/350°F/Gas Mark 4. Grease two 20-cm/8-inch round sandwich tins and line the bases with baking paper. Sift together the plain flour, bicarbonate of soda, cocoa powder and salt.

Place the butter, white vegetable fat and sugar in a large bowl and beat with an electric whisk until pale and fluffy. Beat in the egg and vanilla extract followed by half the flour mixture and then the milk. Stir in the rest of the flour mixture and mix until thoroughly incorporated.

Divide the mixture evenly between the prepared tins and gently level the surfaces. Bake in the preheated oven for 20–25 minutes until risen and just firm to the touch. Cool in the tins for 10 minutes and then remove from the tins and transfer to a wire rack and leave to cool completely.

For the filling, place the marshmallows and milk in a heatproof bowl set over a pan of simmering water. Leave until the marshmallows have melted, stirring occasionally. Remove from the heat and leave to cool.

In a separate bowl whip the cream until holding firm peaks. Fold the cream into the marshmallow mixture. Cover and chill in the refrigerator for 30 minutes.

Sandwich the cakes together with the jam and marshmallow cream. Dust the top of the cake with icing sugar and add birthday candles to decorate.

halloween whoopie pies

makes 8

250 g/9 oz plain flour

1 tsp bicarbonate of soda

1½ tsp mixed spice

large pinch of salt

115 g/4 oz butter, softened

150 g/5½ oz light brown soft sugar

1 large egg, beaten

150 ml/5 fl oz buttermilk

225 g/8 oz orange ready-to-roll fondant icing

icing sugar, for dusting

115 g/4 oz black ready-to-roll fondant icing

tubes of yellow and black writing icing

orange buttercream filling

115 g/4 oz unsalted butter, softened

finely grated rind and juice of 1 small orange

200 g/7 oz icing sugar, sifted

orange food colouring paste

Preheat the oven to 180°C/350°F/Gas Mark 4. Line 2–3 large baking sheets with baking paper. Sift together the plain flour, bicarbonate of soda, mixed spice and salt.

Place the butter and sugar in a large bowl and beat with an electric whisk until pale and fluffy. Beat in the egg followed by half the flour mixture then the buttermilk. Stir in the rest of the flour mixture and mix until thoroughly incorporated.

Pipe or spoon 16 large mounds of the mixture onto the prepared baking sheets, spaced well apart to allow for spreading. Bake in the preheated oven, one sheet at a time, for 11–13 minutes until risen and just firm to the touch. Cool for 5 minutes then using a palette knife transfer to a wire rack and leave to cool completely.

For the filling, place the butter, orange rind and juice in a bowl and beat with an electric whisk for 2–3 minutes until pale and creamy. Gradually beat in the icing sugar and continue beating for 2–3 minutes until the buttercream is very light and fluffy. Beat in a little orange colouring paste to colour the buttercream bright orange.

To assemble, spread or pipe the buttercream onto the flat side of half of the cakes. Top with the remaining cakes. Thinly roll the orange fondant icing out on a surface dusted with icing sugar and cut out eight rounds to fit the top of the cakes. Press gently onto the cakes. Roll out the black icing and cut out four bat shapes. Place on half the cakes and use yellow writing icing to dot eyes on the bats. Use black writing icing to pipe spider's webs on the remaining cakes.

snowflake christmas whoopie pies

makes 14

200 g/7 oz plain flour

2 tsp baking powder

large pinch of salt

55 g/2 oz ground almonds

115 g/4 oz butter, softened

150 g/5½ oz caster sugar, plus extra for sprinkling

1 large egg, beaten

1 tsp almond extract

100 ml/3½ fl oz milk

1 tbsp edible silver balls

buttercream filling

150 g/5½ oz unsalted butter, softened

8 tbsp double cream

280 g/10 oz icing sugar, sifted

icing

115 g/4 oz icing sugar

1–2 tbsp warm water

Preheat the oven to 180°C/350°F/Gas Mark 4. Line 2–3 large baking sheets with baking paper. Sift together the plain flour, baking powder and salt. Stir in the ground almonds.

Place the butter and sugar in a large bowl and beat with an electric whisk until pale and fluffy. Beat in the egg and almond extract followed by half the flour mixture then the milk. Stir in the rest of the flour mixture and beat until thoroughly incorporated.

Pipe or spoon 28 mounds of the mixture onto the prepared baking sheets, spaced well apart to allow for spreading. Bake in the preheated oven, one sheet at a time, for 10–12 minutes until risen and just firm to the touch. Cool for 5 minutes then using a palette knife transfer to a wire rack and leave to cool completely.

For the filling, place the butter in a bowl and beat with an electric whisk for 2–3 minutes until pale and creamy. Beat in the cream then gradually beat in the icing sugar and continue beating for 2–3 minutes until the buttercream is very light and fluffy.

For the icing, sift the icing sugar into a bowl and gradually stir in enough water to make a smooth, thick icing that is thick enough to coat the back of a wooden spoon.

To assemble, spread or pipe the buttercream on the flat side of half of the cakes. Top with the rest of the cakes. Spoon the icing into a small paper piping bag, snip the end and pipe snowflake patterns on the top of the whoopie pies. Decorate with silver balls and sprinkle with caster sugar. Leave to set.

chocolate fudge
brownie whoopie pies

makes 18

175 g/6 oz plain flour

¾ tsp bicarbonate of soda

25 g/1 oz cocoa powder

pinch of salt

100 g/3½ oz butter, softened

125 g/4½ oz soft dark brown
sugar

1 large egg, beaten

1 tsp vanilla extract

4 tbsp buttermilk

25 g/1 oz plain chocolate, finely
chopped

40 g/1½ oz pecan nuts, finely
chopped

chocolate fudge
frosting

55 g/2 oz unsalted butter

85 g/3 oz plain chocolate, broken
into pieces

115 g/4 oz soft light brown sugar

2 tbsp milk

175 g/6 oz icing sugar, sifted

Preheat the oven to 180°C/350°F/Gas Mark 4. Line 2–3 large baking sheets with baking paper. Sift together the plain flour, bicarbonate of soda, cocoa powder and salt.

Place the butter and sugar in a large bowl and beat with an electric whisk until pale and fluffy. Whisk in the egg and vanilla extract followed by half the flour mixture then the buttermilk. Stir in the rest of the flour mixture and mix until thoroughly incorporated. Stir in the chocolate and 25 g/1 oz of the pecan nuts.

Pipe or spoon 36 small mounds of the mixture onto the prepared baking sheets, spaced well apart to allow for spreading. Bake in the preheated oven, one sheet at a time, for 8–10 minutes until risen and just firm to the touch. Cool for 5 minutes then using a palette knife transfer to a wire rack and leave to cool completely.

For the frosting, place the butter, chocolate, brown sugar and milk in a pan and heat gently until the sugar dissolves, then bring to the boil and boil for 2–3 minutes. Remove from the heat and gradually beat in the icing sugar until smooth.

To assemble, spread or pipe three-quarters of frosting on the flat side of half the cakes. Top with the rest of the cakes. Swirl the rest of the frosting on top of the whoopie pies and decorate with the reserved pecan nuts.

blueberry cheesecake whoopie pies

makes 12

250 g/9 oz plain flour

1 tsp bicarbonate of soda

large pinch of salt

115 g/4 oz butter, softened

150 g/5½ oz caster sugar

1 large egg, beaten

1 tsp vanilla extract

4 tbsp soured cream

3 tbsp milk

55 g/2 oz sweetened dried blueberries

icing sugar, for dusting

lemon cheesecake filling

225 g/8 oz full-fat soft cheese

2 tsp finely grated lemon rind

6 tbsp soured cream

40 g/1½ oz icing sugar, sifted

Preheat the oven to 180°C/350°F/Gas Mark 4. Line 2–3 large baking sheets with baking paper. Sift together the plain flour, bicarbonate of soda and salt.

Place the butter and sugar in a large bowl and beat with an electric whisk until pale and fluffy. Whisk in the egg and vanilla extract followed by half the flour mixture then the soured cream and milk. Stir in the rest of the flour mixture and mix until thoroughly incorporated. Stir in the blueberries.

Pipe or spoon 24 mounds of the mixture onto the prepared baking sheets, spaced well apart to allow for spreading. Bake in the preheated oven, one sheet at a time, for 10–12 minutes until risen and just firm to the touch. Cool for 5 minutes then using a palette knife transfer to a wire rack and leave to cool completely.

For the filling, place the soft cheese, lemon rind, soured cream and icing sugar in a bowl and beat together until smooth.

To assemble, spread or pipe the lemon filling on the flat side of half the cakes. Top with the rest of the cakes and dust lightly with icing sugar.

pina colada whoopie pies

makes 12

225 g/8 oz plain flour

2 tsp baking powder

large pinch of salt

55 g/2 oz desiccated coconut

115 g/4 oz butter, softened

150 g/5½ oz caster sugar

1 large egg, beaten

100 ml/3½ fl oz milk

25 g/1 oz crystallized pineapple,
finely chopped

toasted coconut shavings, to
decorate

rum cream filling

300 ml/10 fl oz double cream

2 tbsp white rum

icing

115 g/4 oz icing sugar

1–2 tbsp pineapple juice

Preheat the oven to 180°C/350°F/Gas Mark 4. Line 2–3 large baking sheets with baking paper. Sift together the plain flour, baking powder and salt. Stir in the coconut.

Place the butter and sugar in a large bowl and beat with an electric whisk until pale and fluffy. Beat in the egg followed by half the flour mixture then the milk. Stir in the rest of the flour mixture and mix until thoroughly incorporated. Fold in the chopped pineapple.

Pipe or spoon 24 mounds of the mixture onto the prepared baking sheets, spaced well apart to allow for spreading. Bake in the preheated oven, one sheet at a time, for 10–12 minutes until risen and just firm to the touch. Cool for 5 minutes then using a palette knife transfer to a wire rack and leave to cool completely.

For the filling, place the cream and rum in a bowl and whip together until holding firm peaks.

For the icing, sift the icing sugar into a bowl and gradually stir in enough pineapple juice to make a smooth icing.

To assemble, spread or pipe the rum cream on the flat side of half the cakes. Top with the rest of the cakes. Spoon the icing over the whoopie pies letting it drip down the sides. Decorate with toasted coconut shavings. Leave to set.